Zen and Friends
A Doodle and Pattern Sketchbook

by Stacy Moody

Zen and Friends
A Doodle and Pattern Sketchbook

ISBN:800104762355

Printed in USA

Zen the Owl and his friends live in a world of doodles and patterns but they need some help. Can you make their world interesting by filling it in with your own doodles and patterns?

What follows are some sample patterns I've created to get you started. On the eight pages after, you are to practice your own patterns. Finally, you help Zen and his friends by completing their world.

I recommend using a pencil and eraser to first create your doodle and pattern frames. Next use a black artist pen to trace your frames and fill in where needed. You can use crayons or colored pencils to color in your designs.

Try using different sizes. I've found that the fine point pens (0.6 mm) work best for me.

Sample Patterns

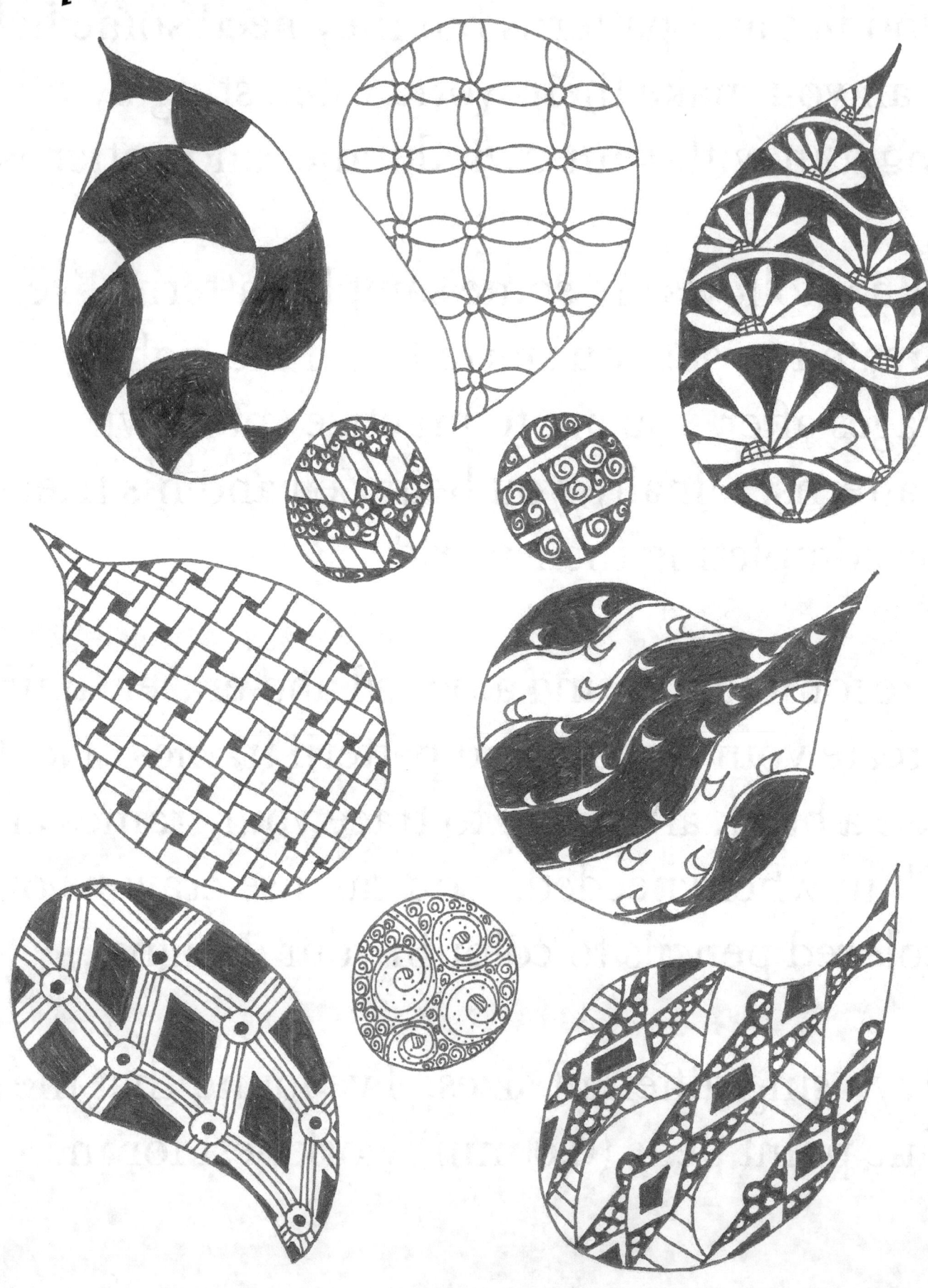

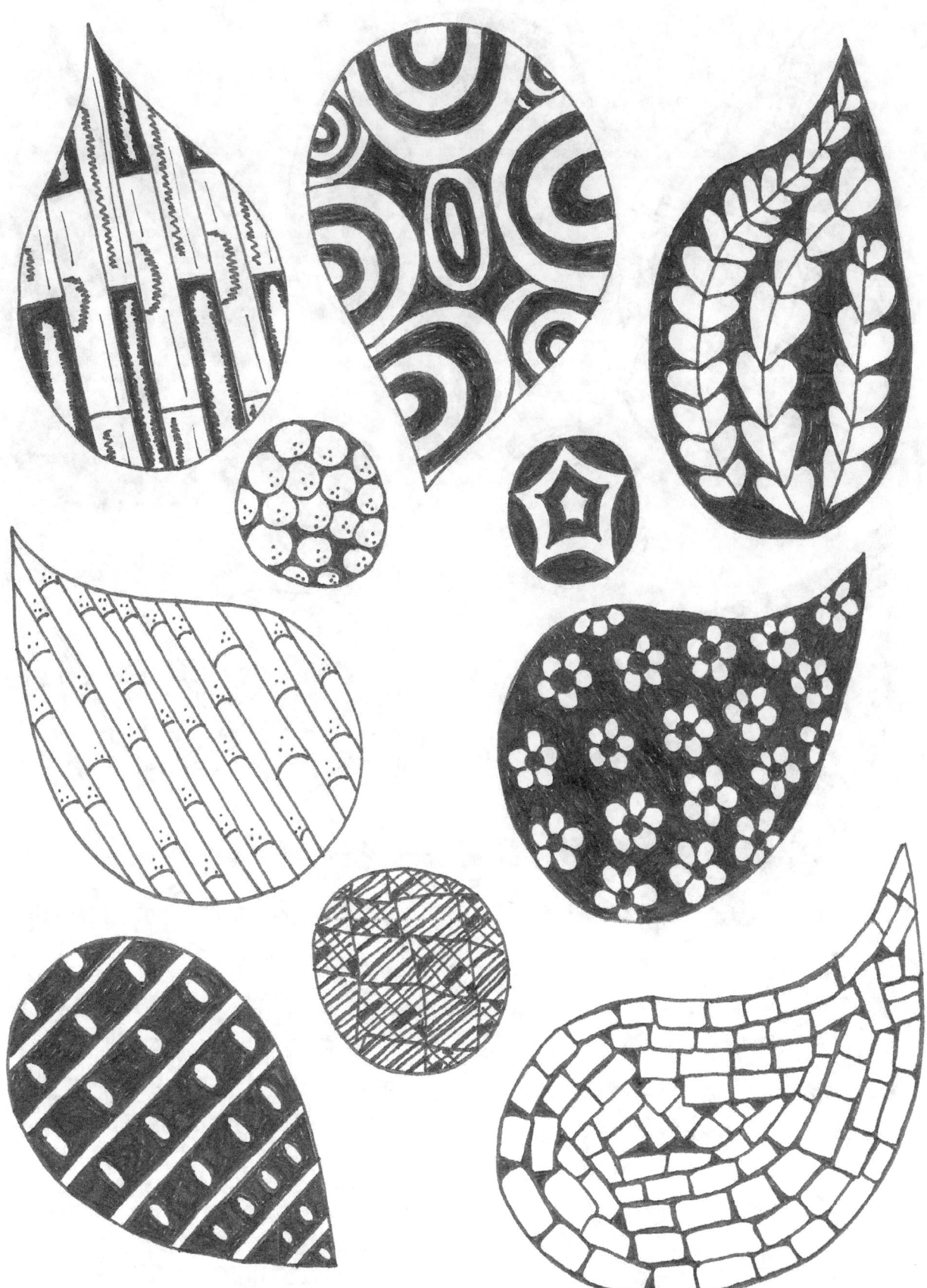

Sample Patterns

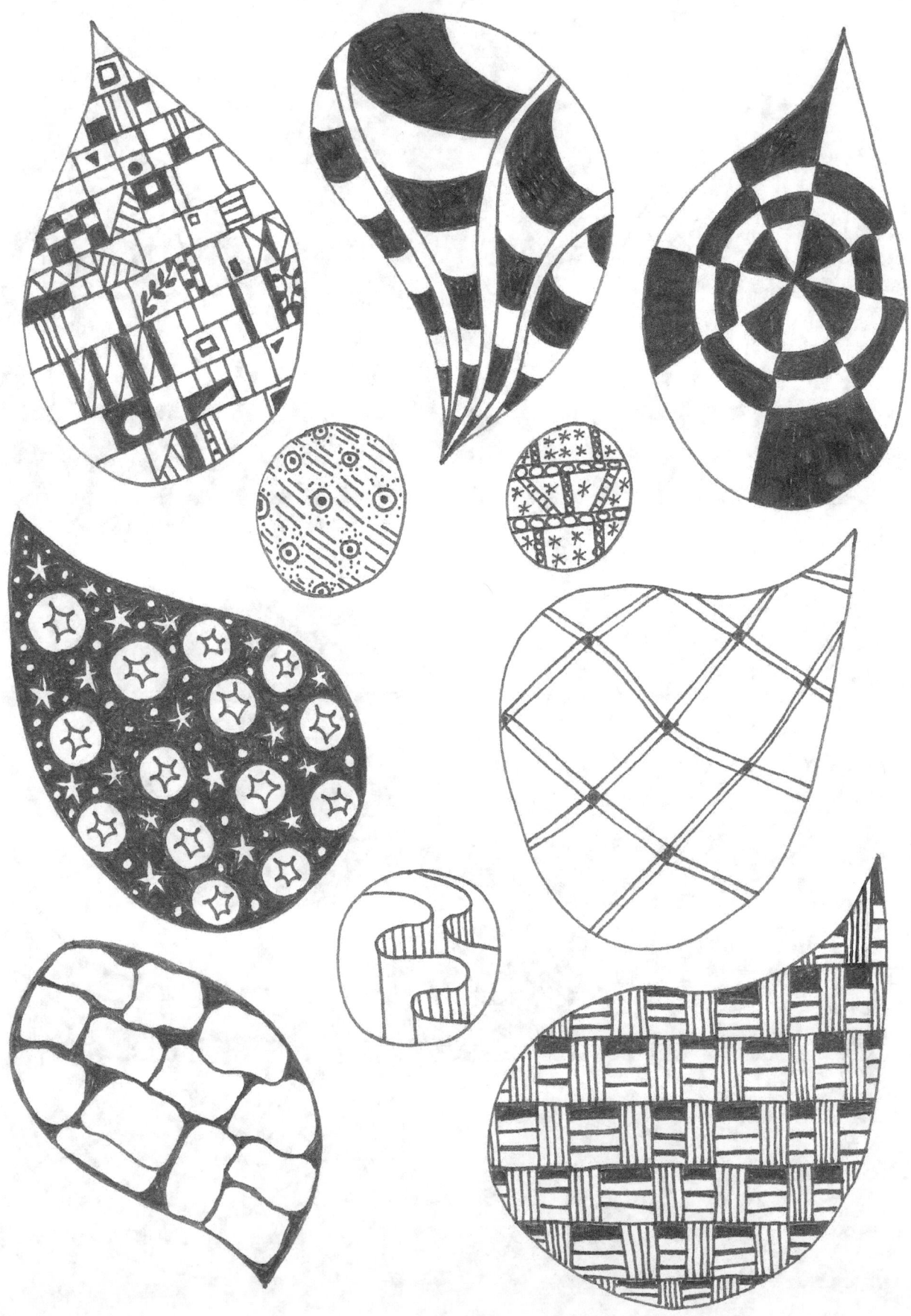

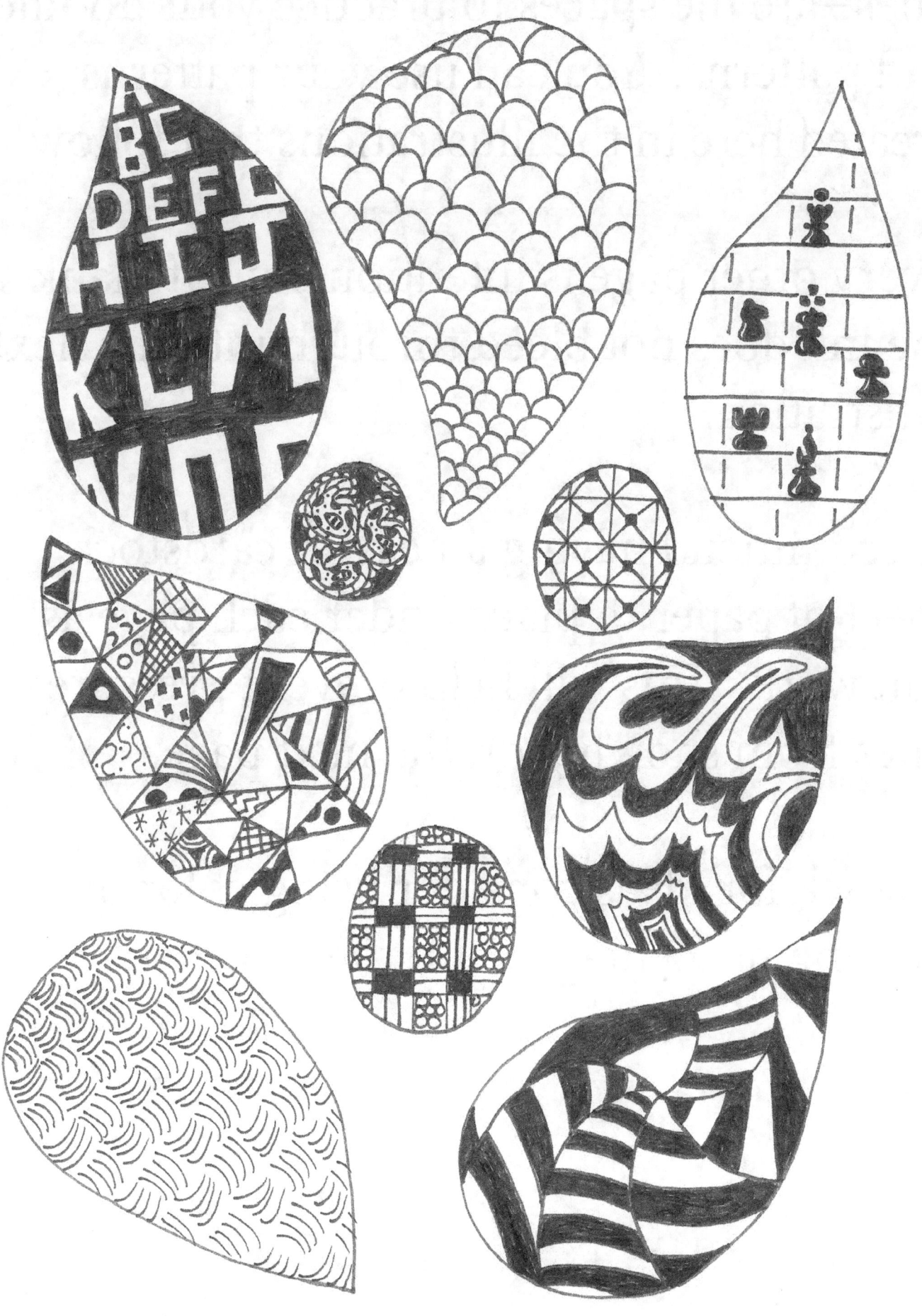

These are the spaces to practice your doodles and patterns. You can use your patterns created here in the illustrations that follow.

Every other page is intentionally left blank so the ink does not bleed through into the next illustration.

I recommend having a heavier cardstock sheet of paper to place under each page as you work. This will help prevent pressure lines from showing on the next page.

If stuck for ideas consider using color or looking up Zentagles® on the Internet.

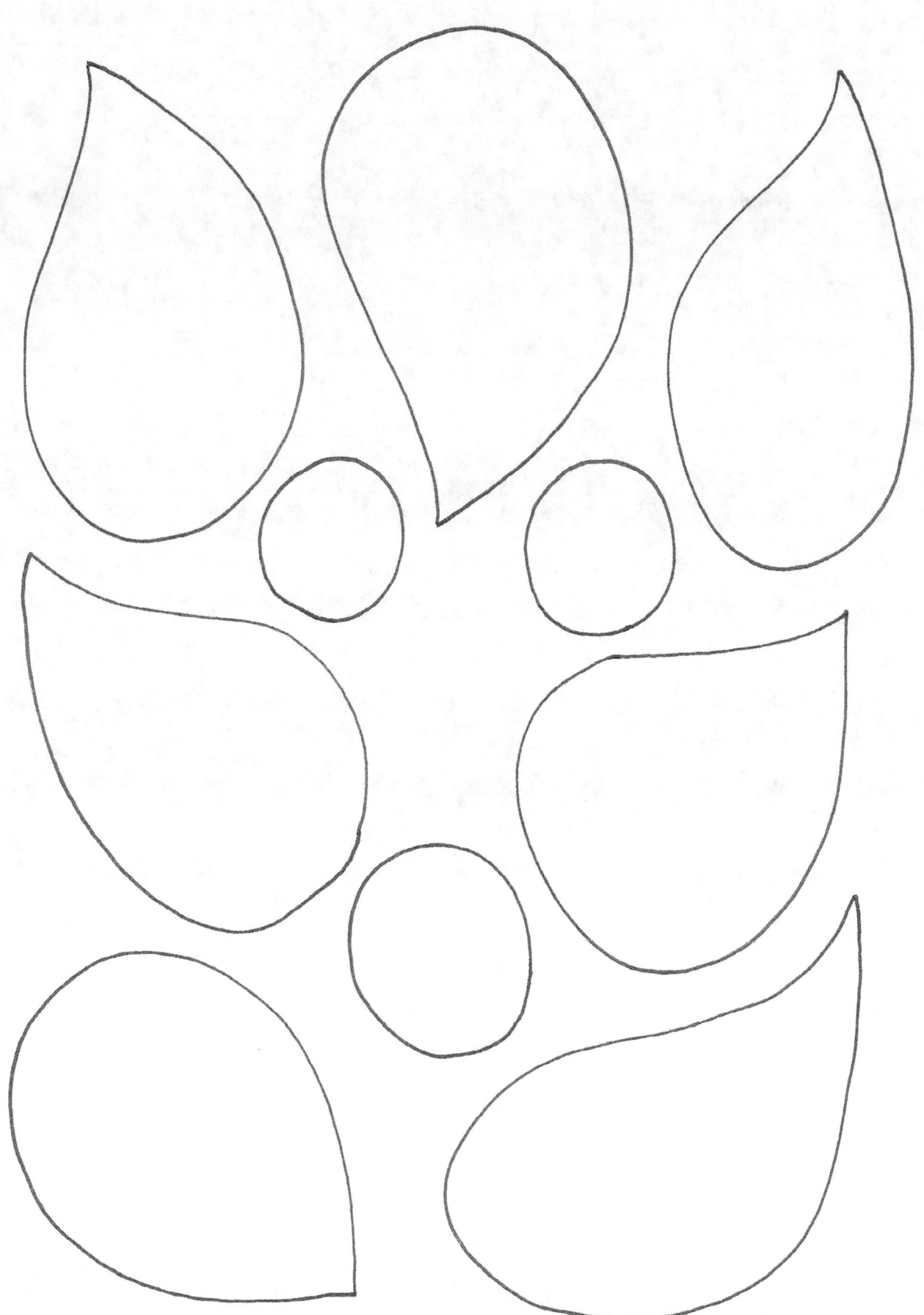

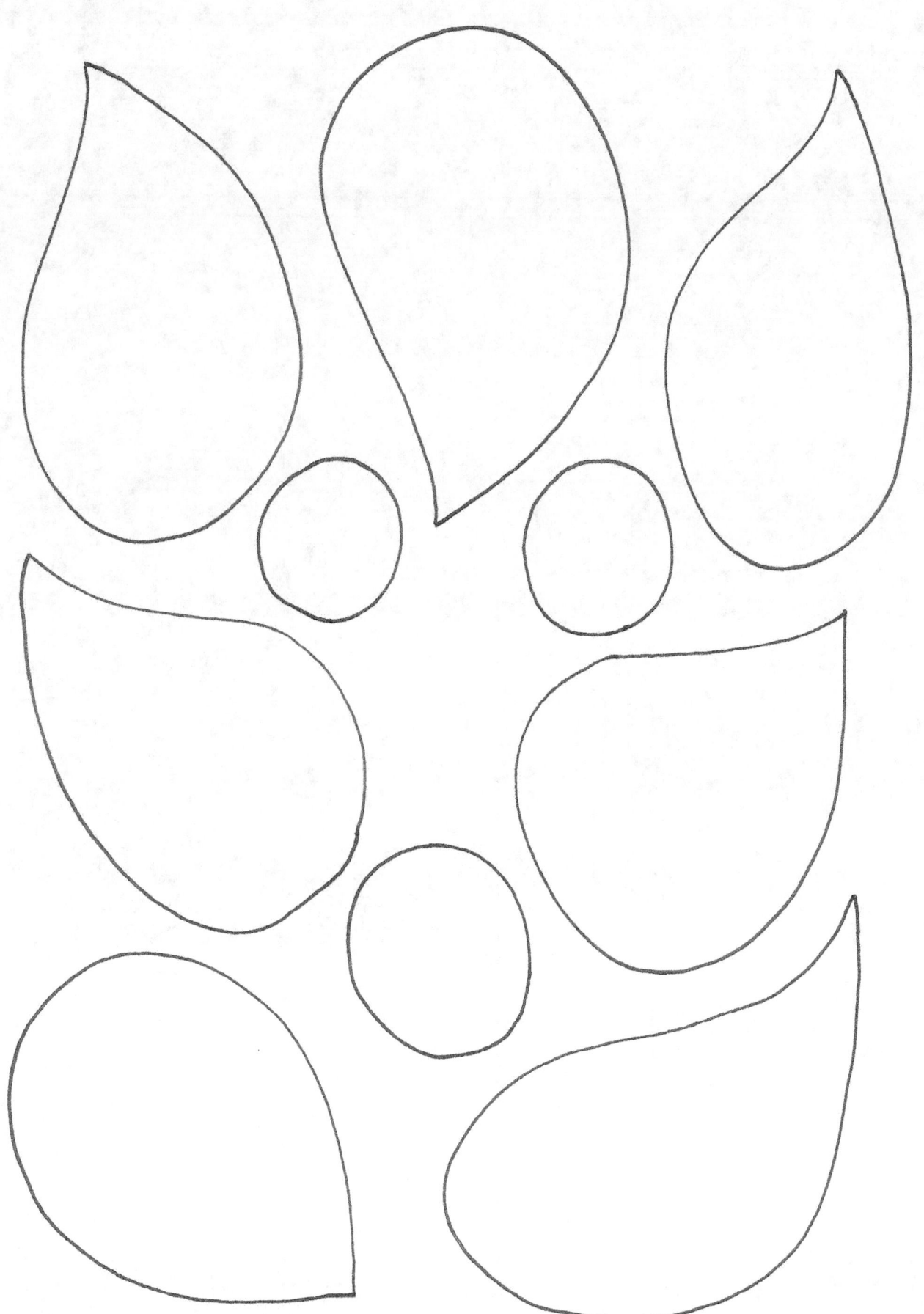

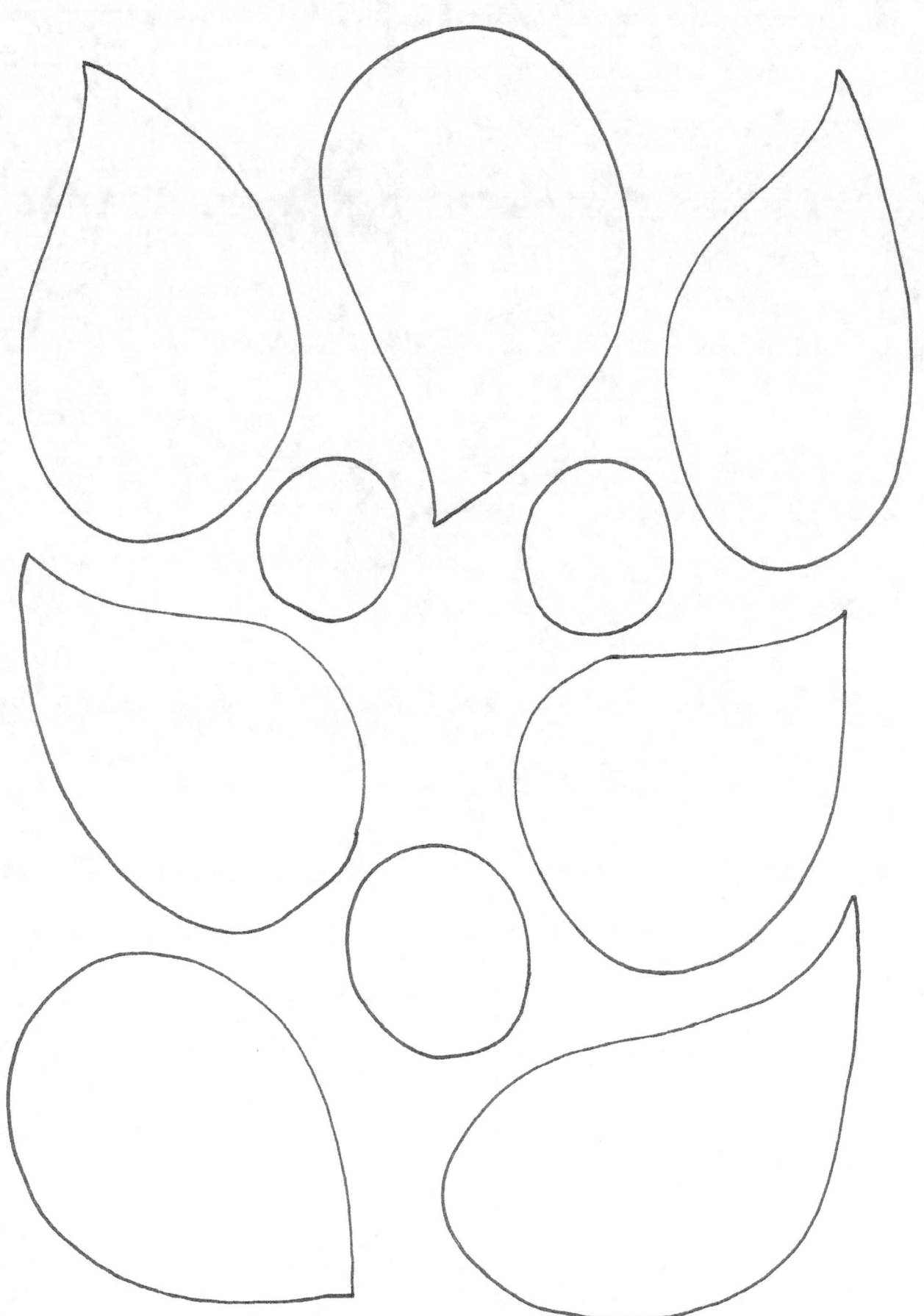

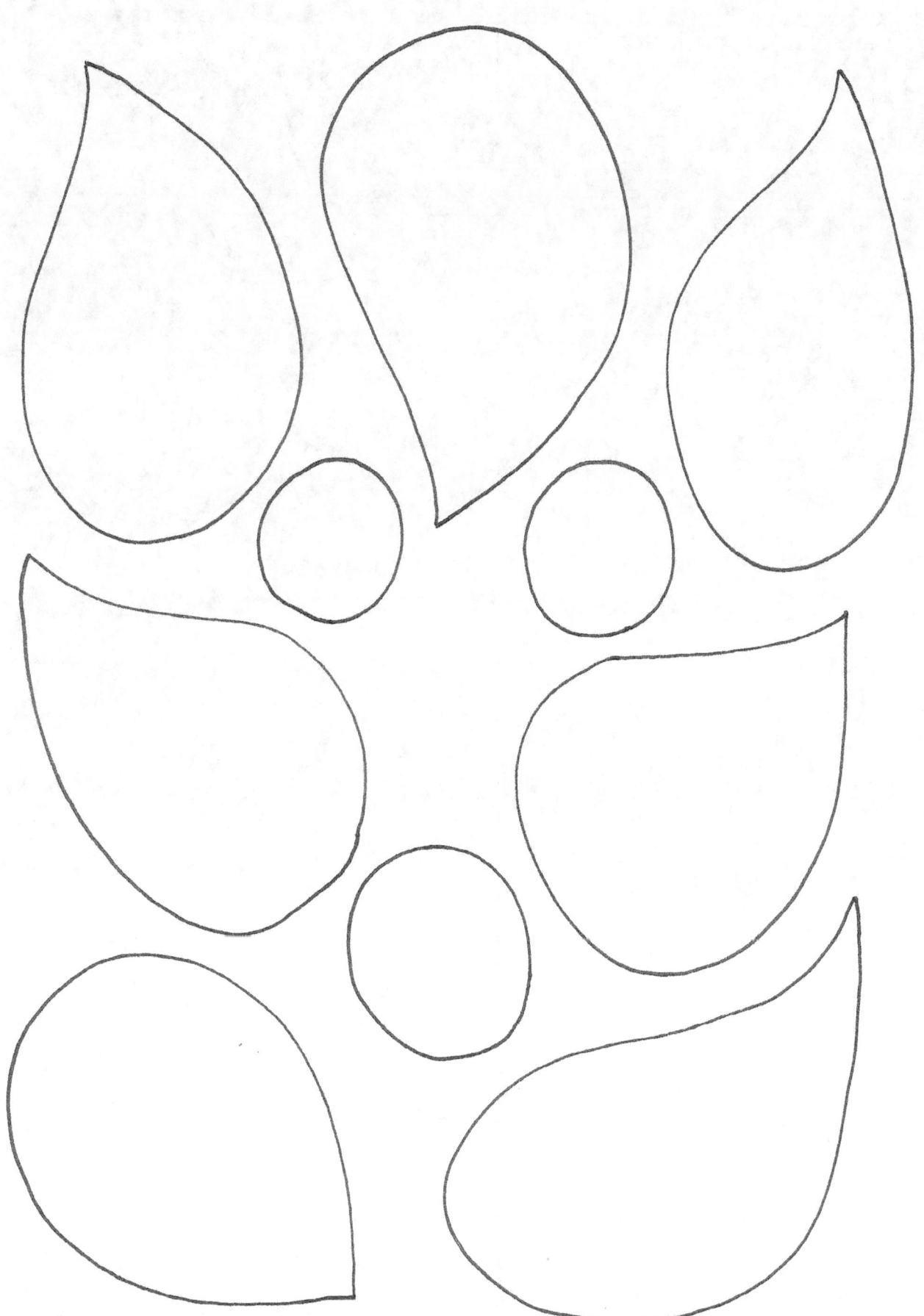

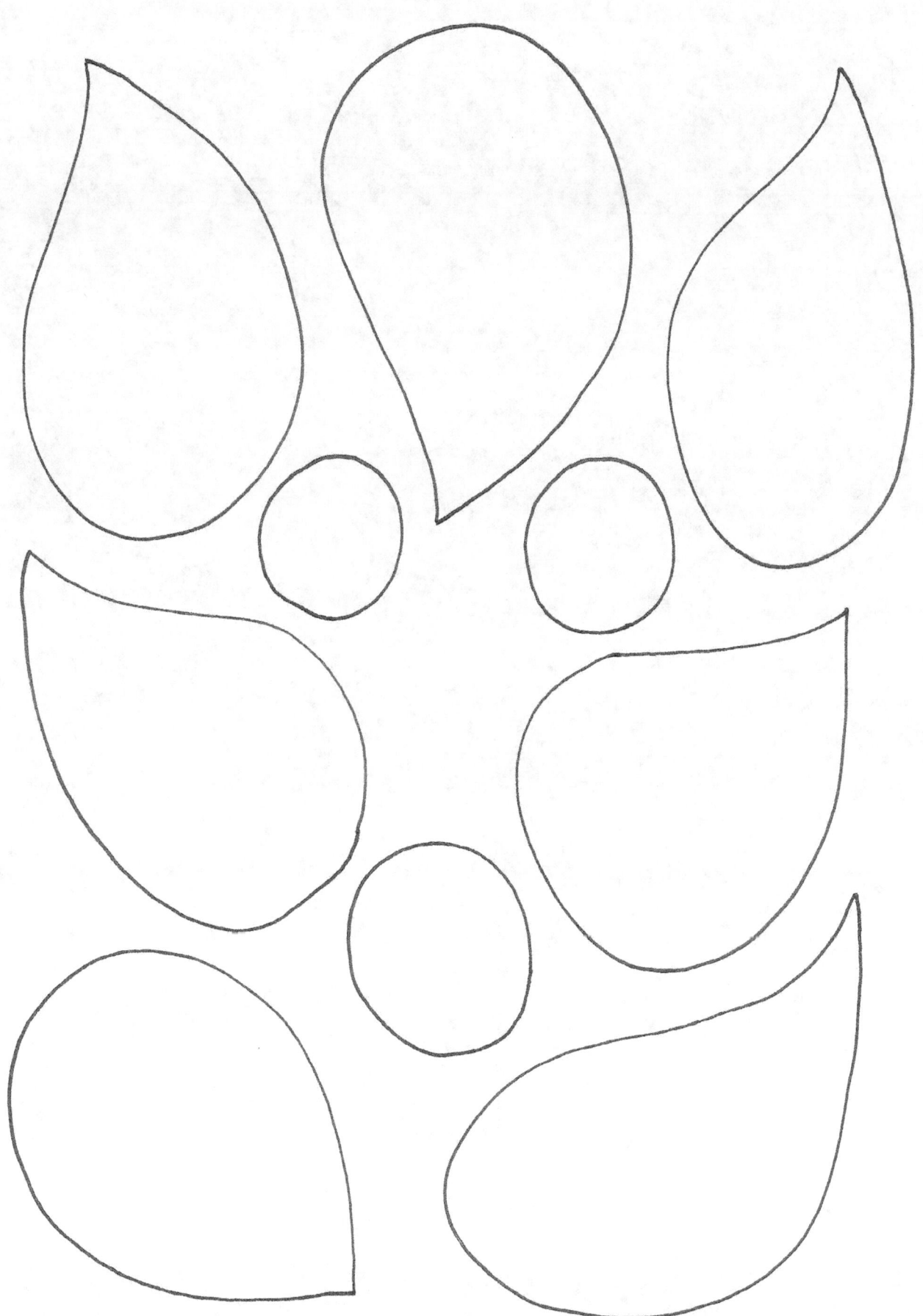

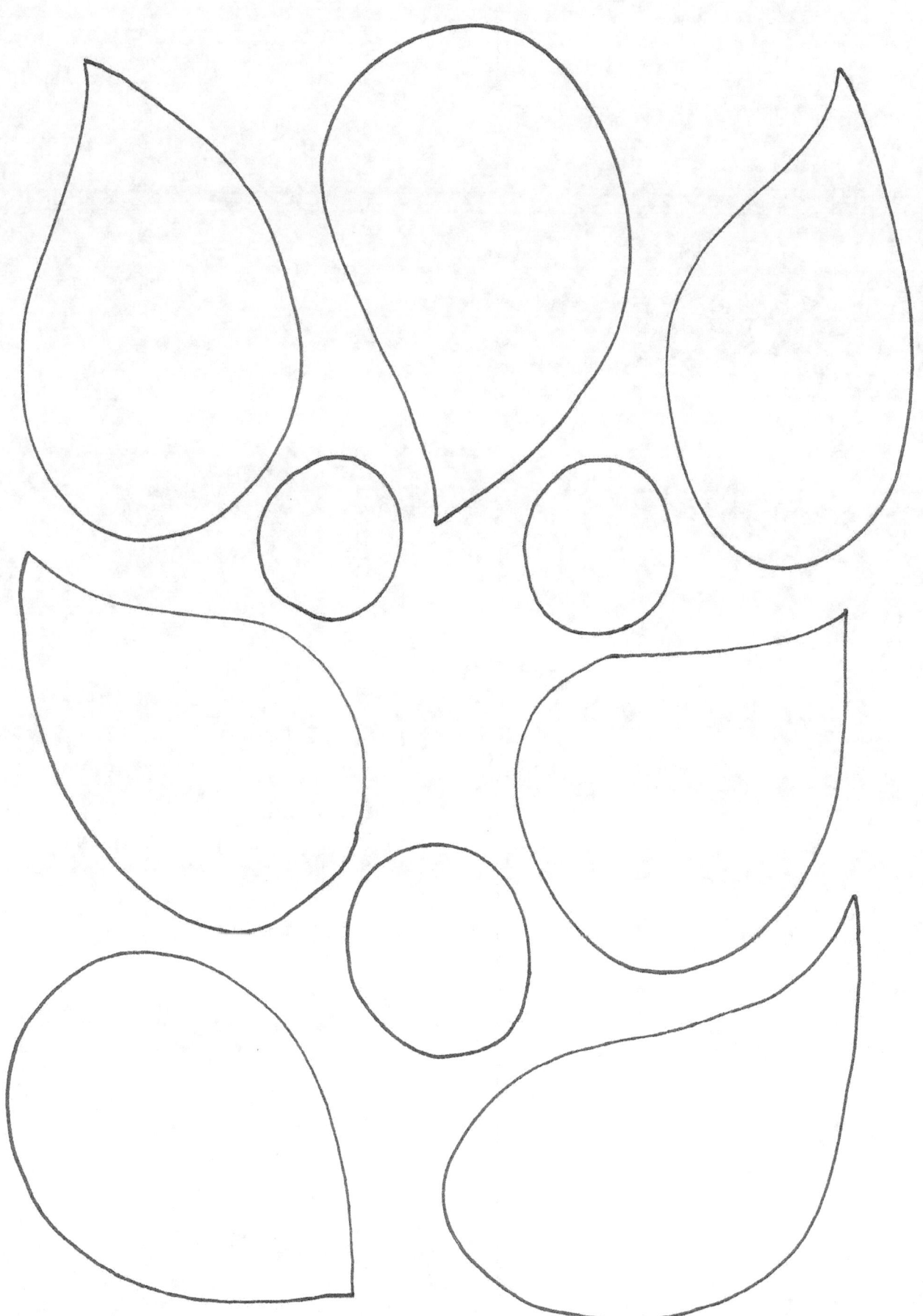

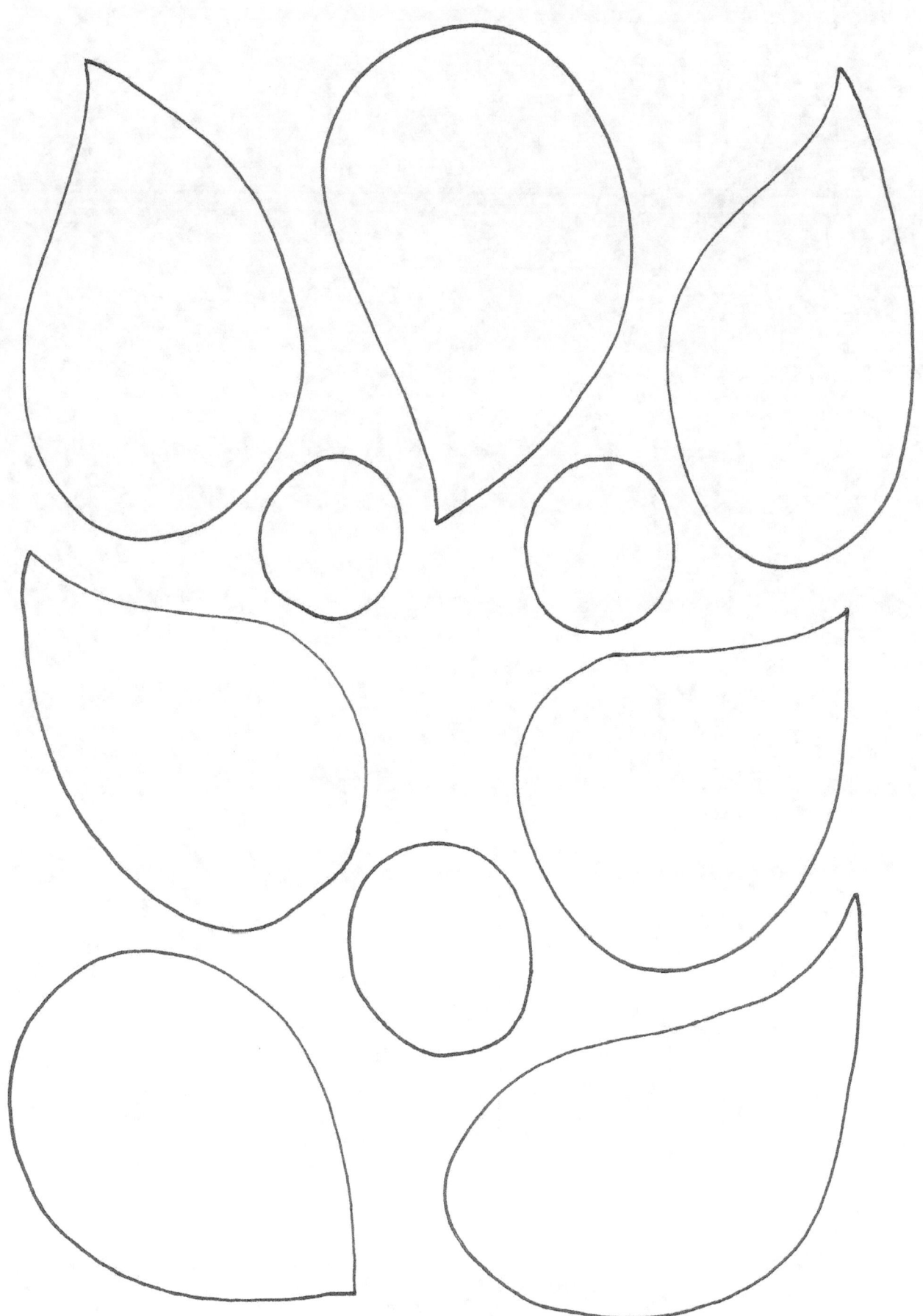

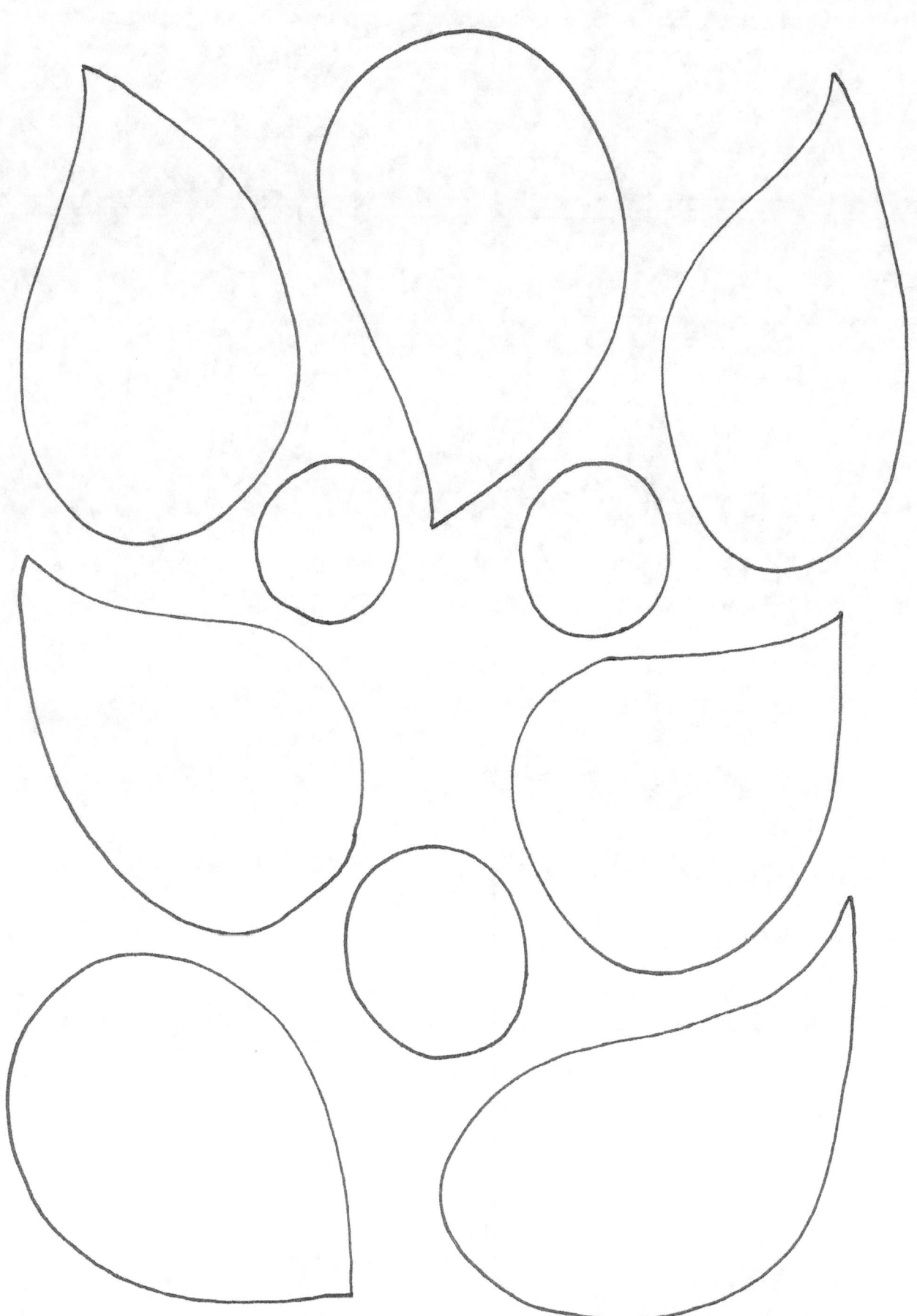

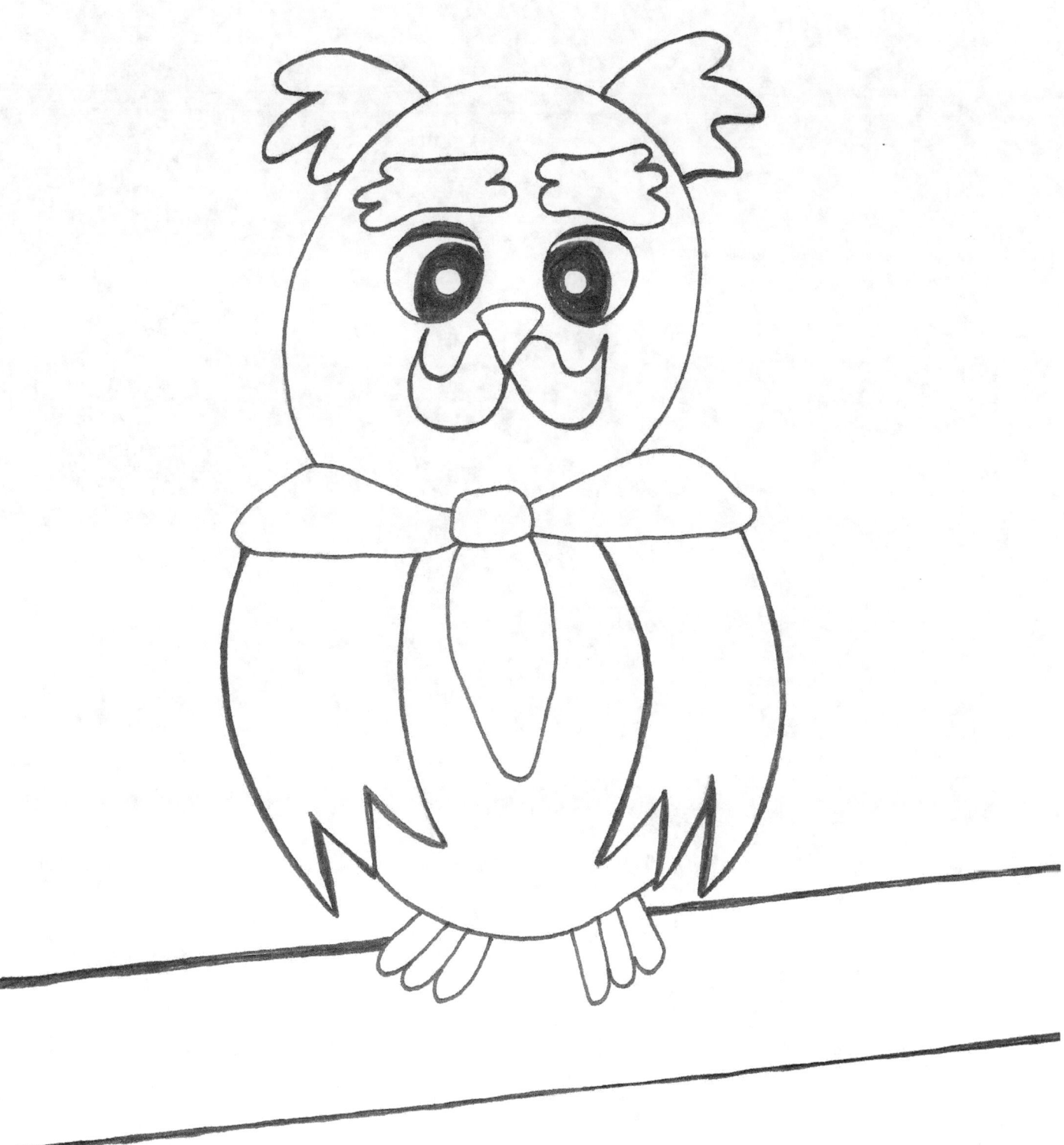

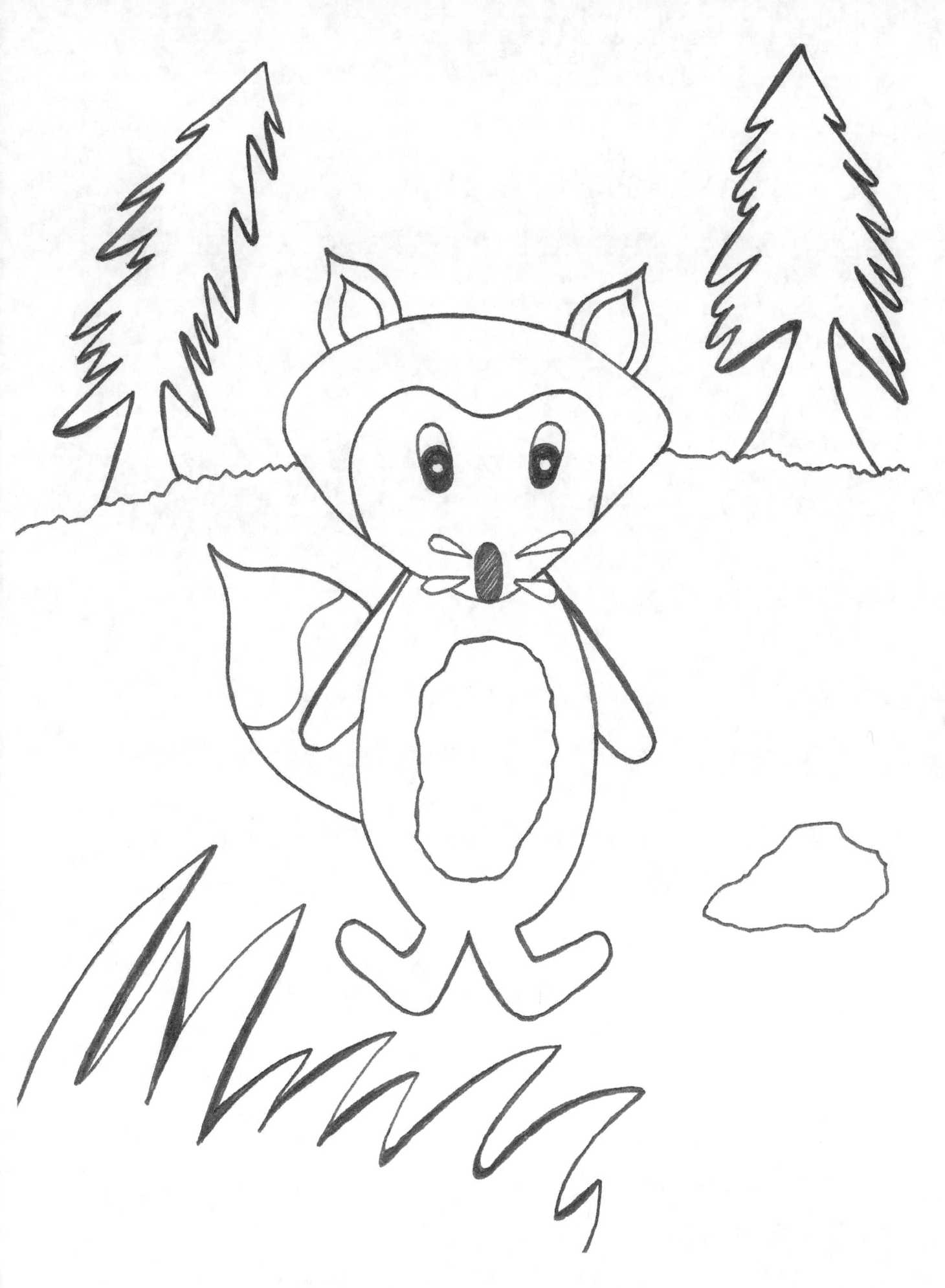

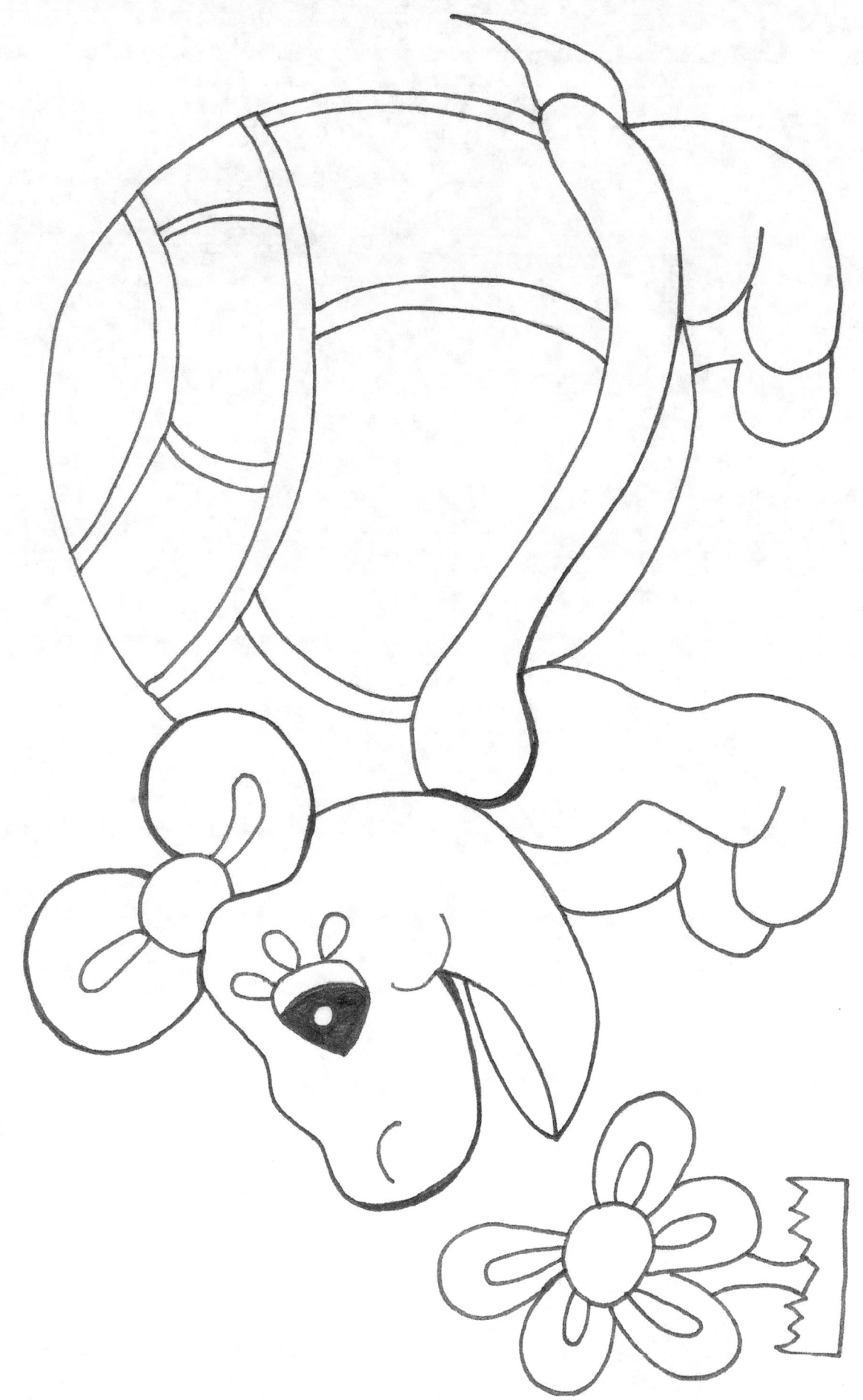

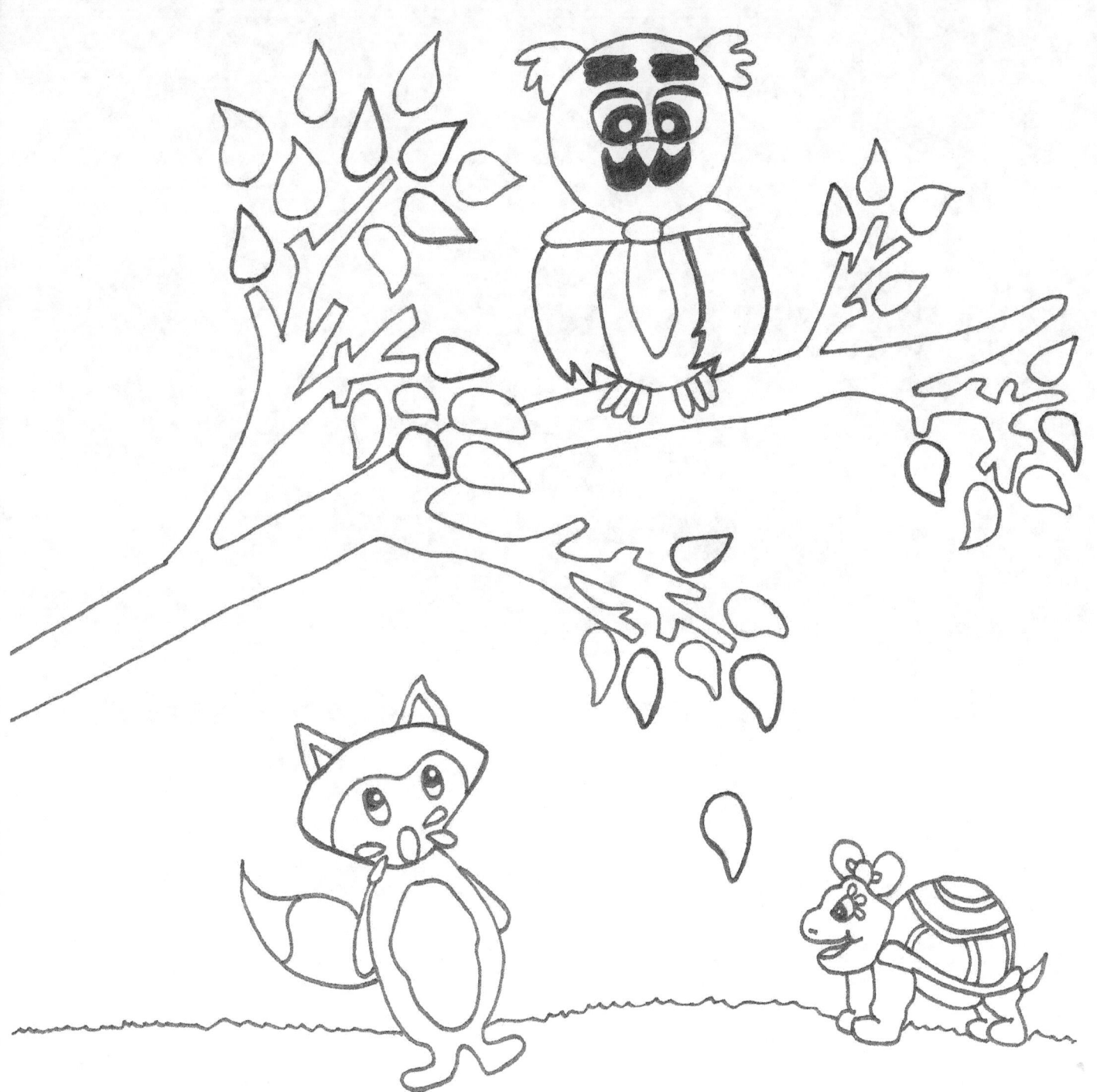

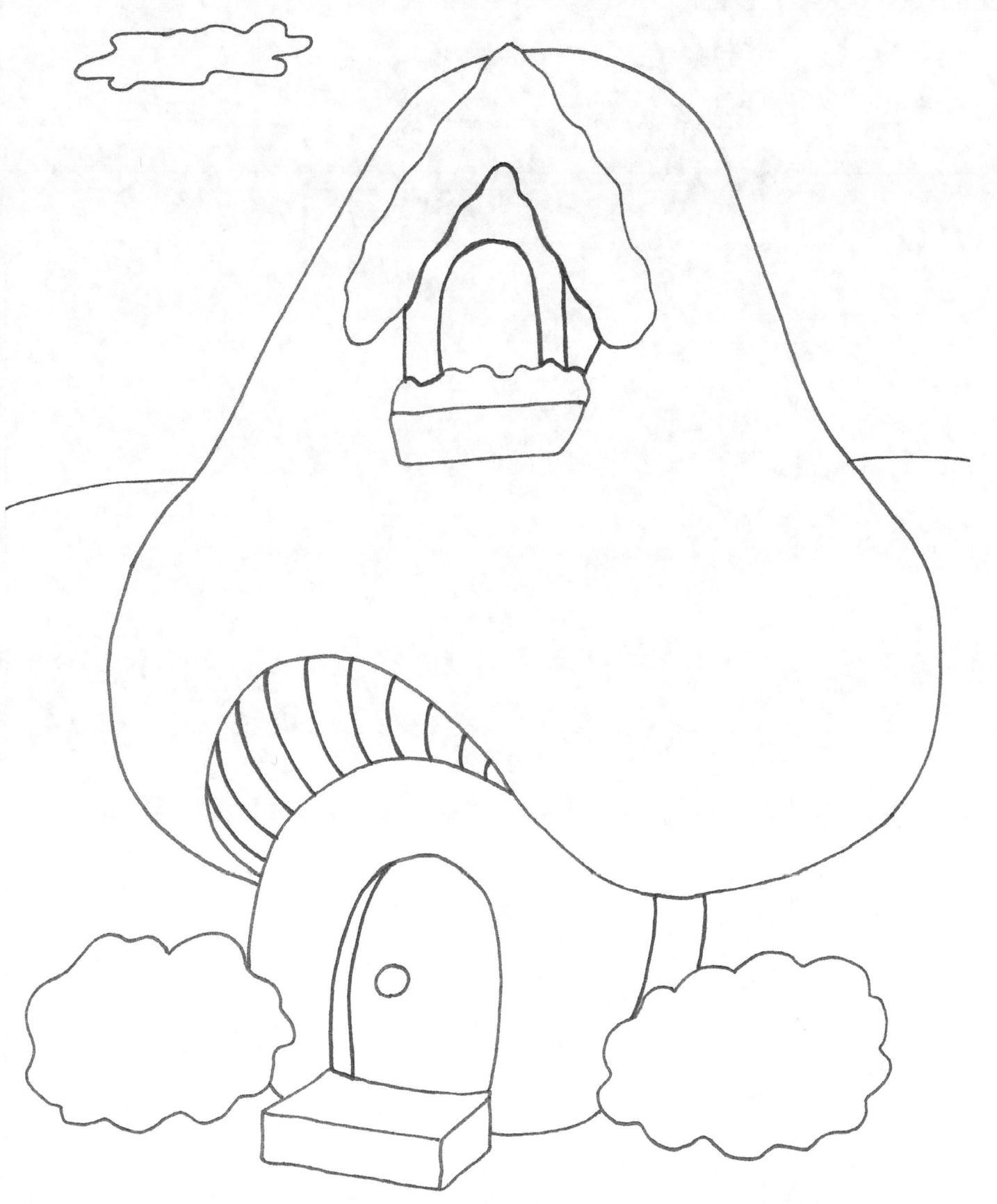

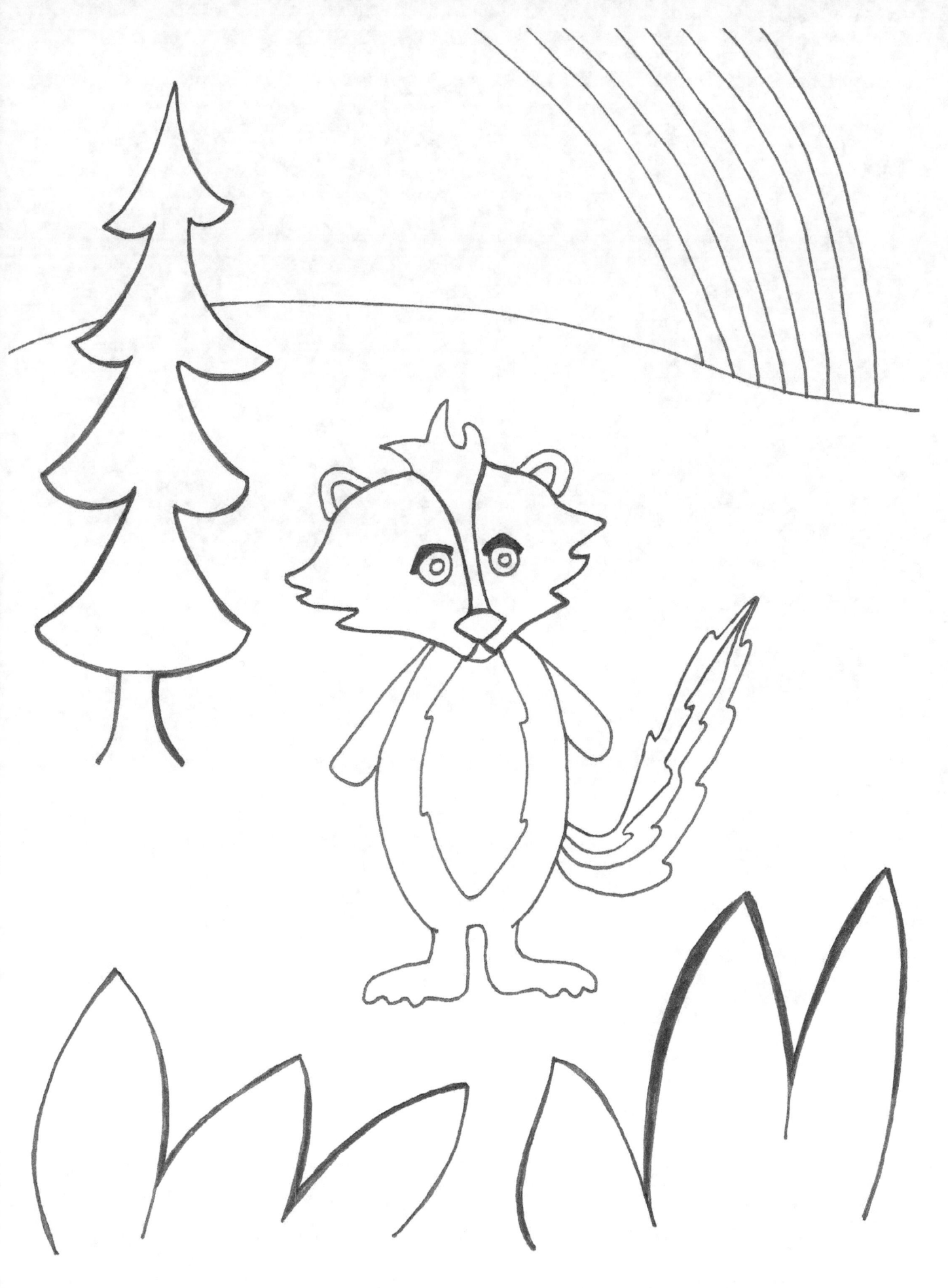

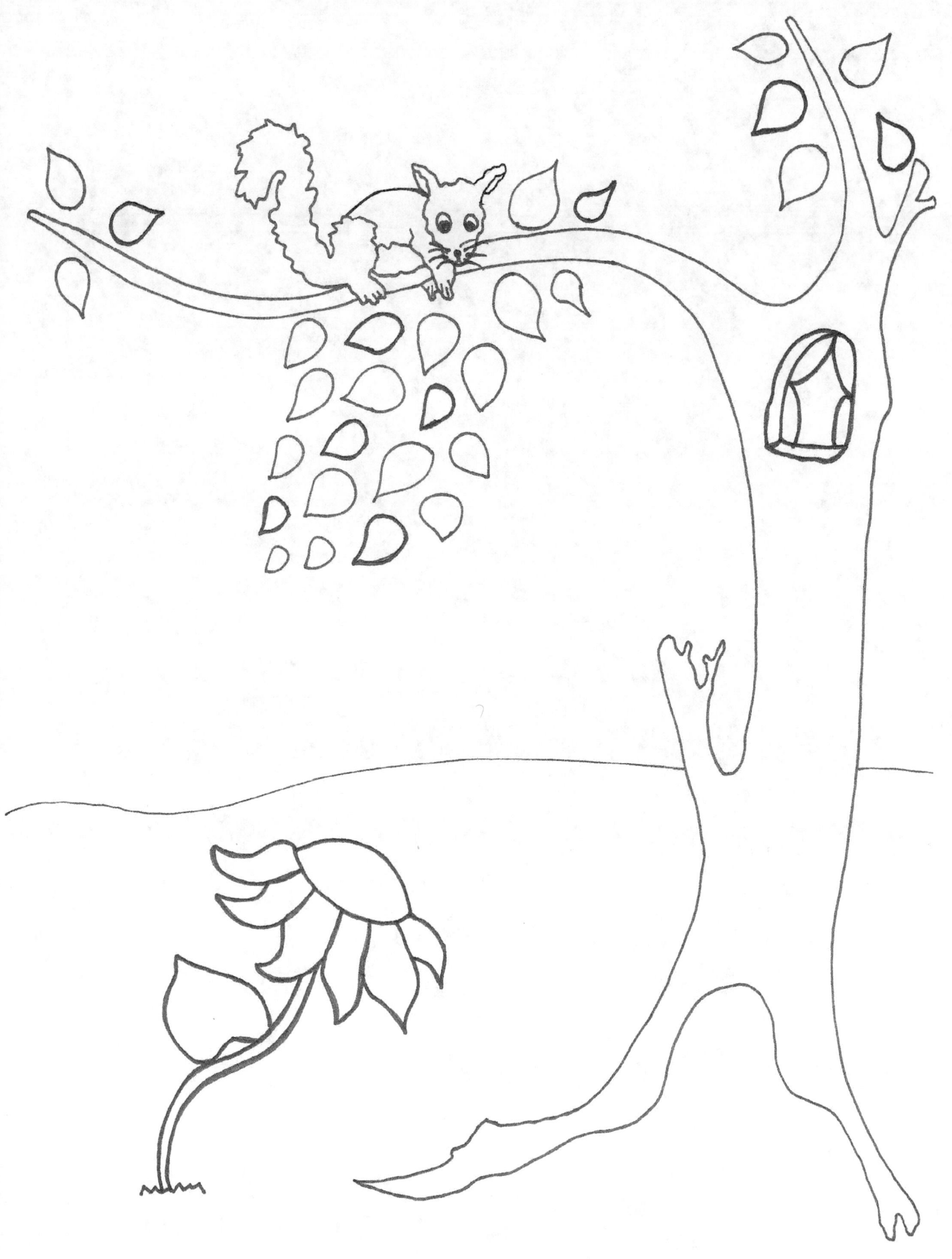

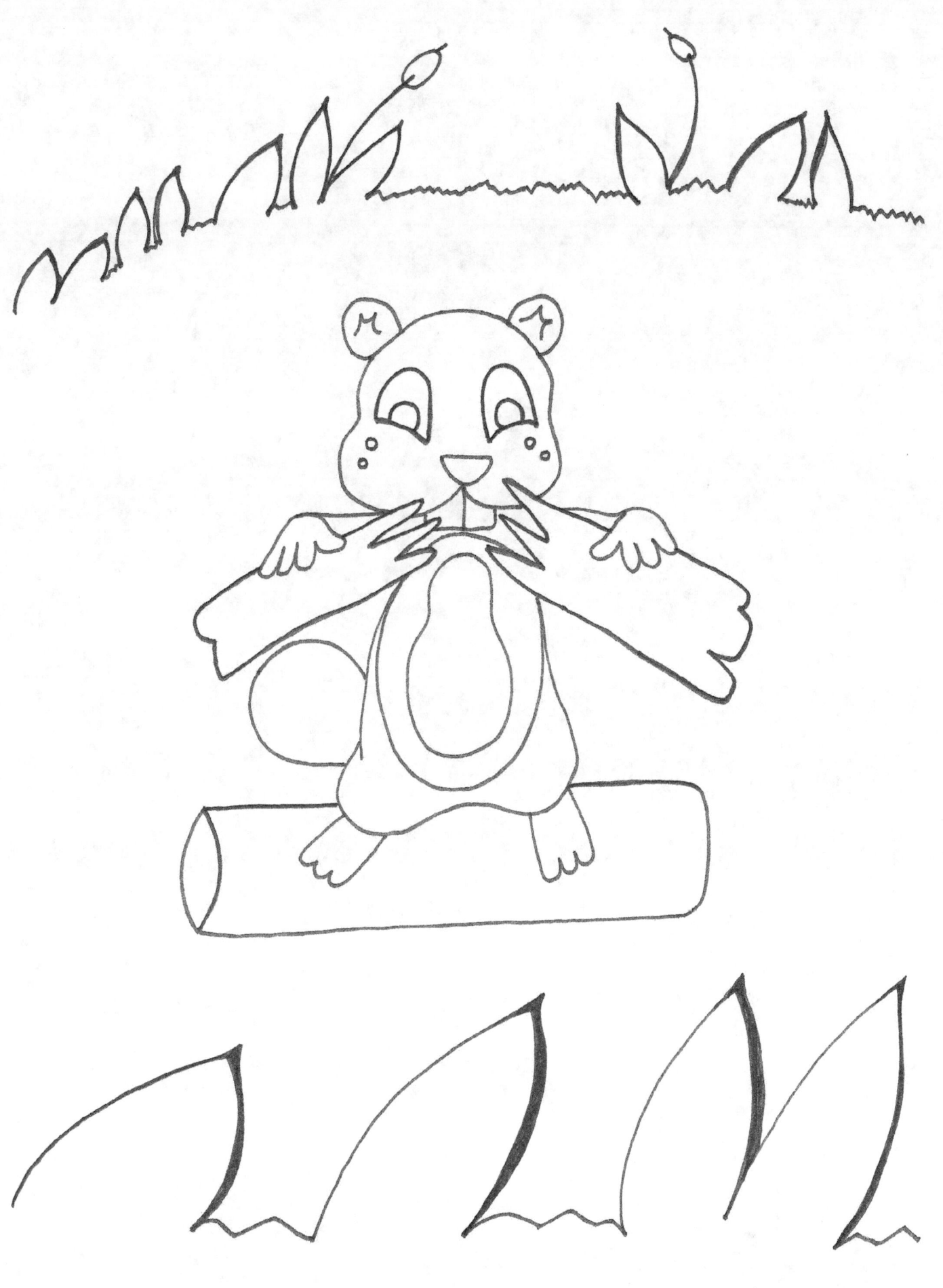

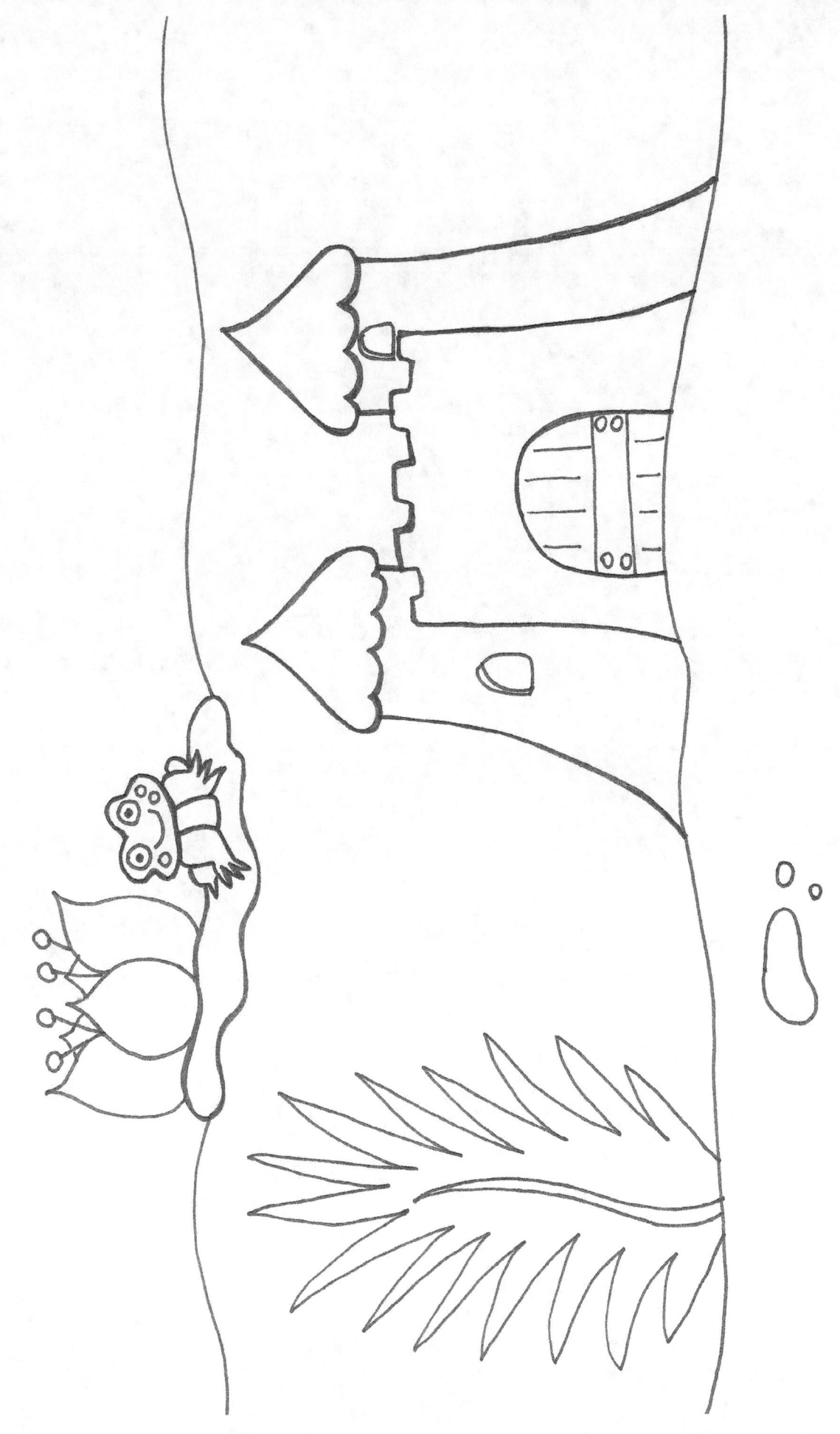

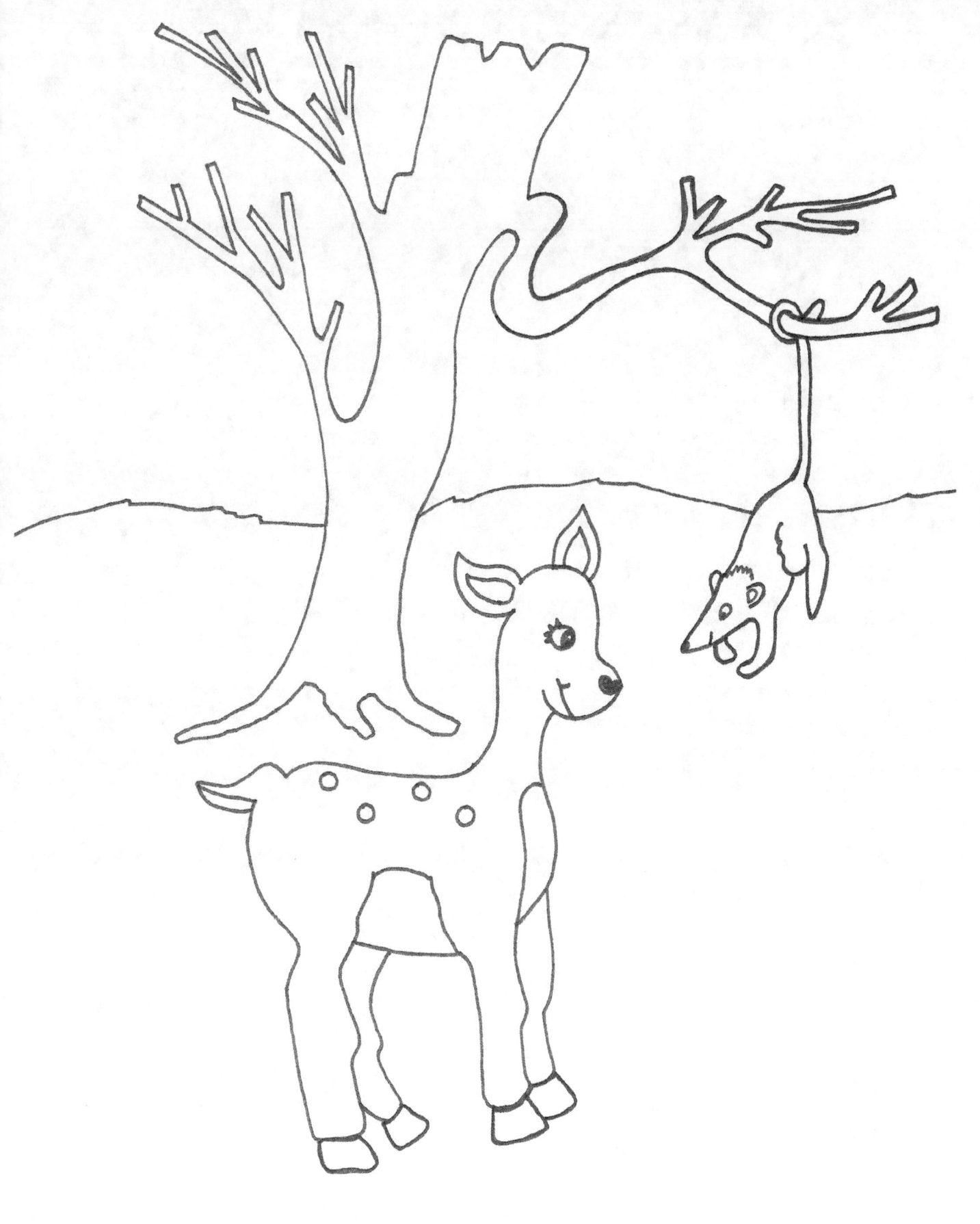

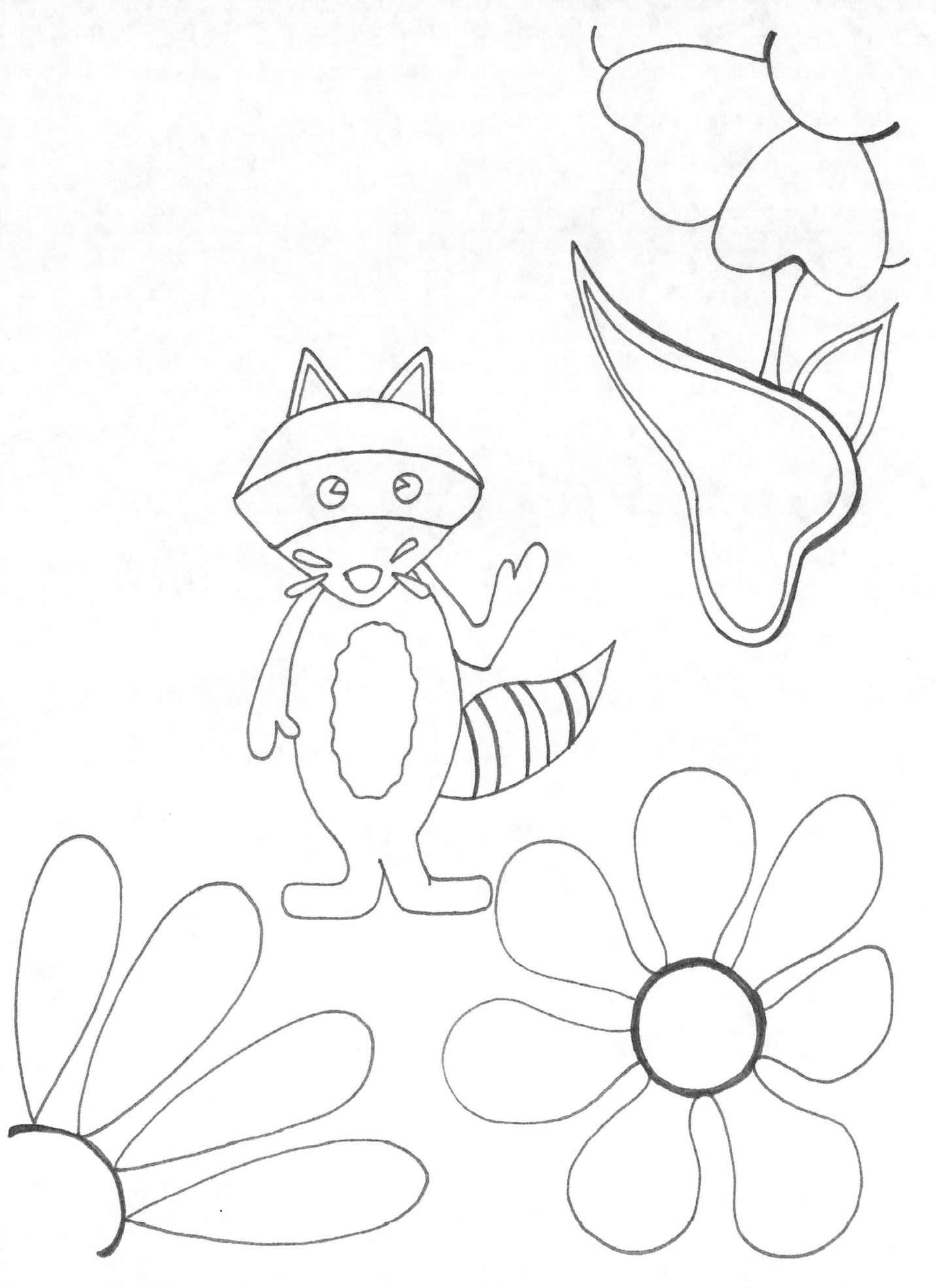

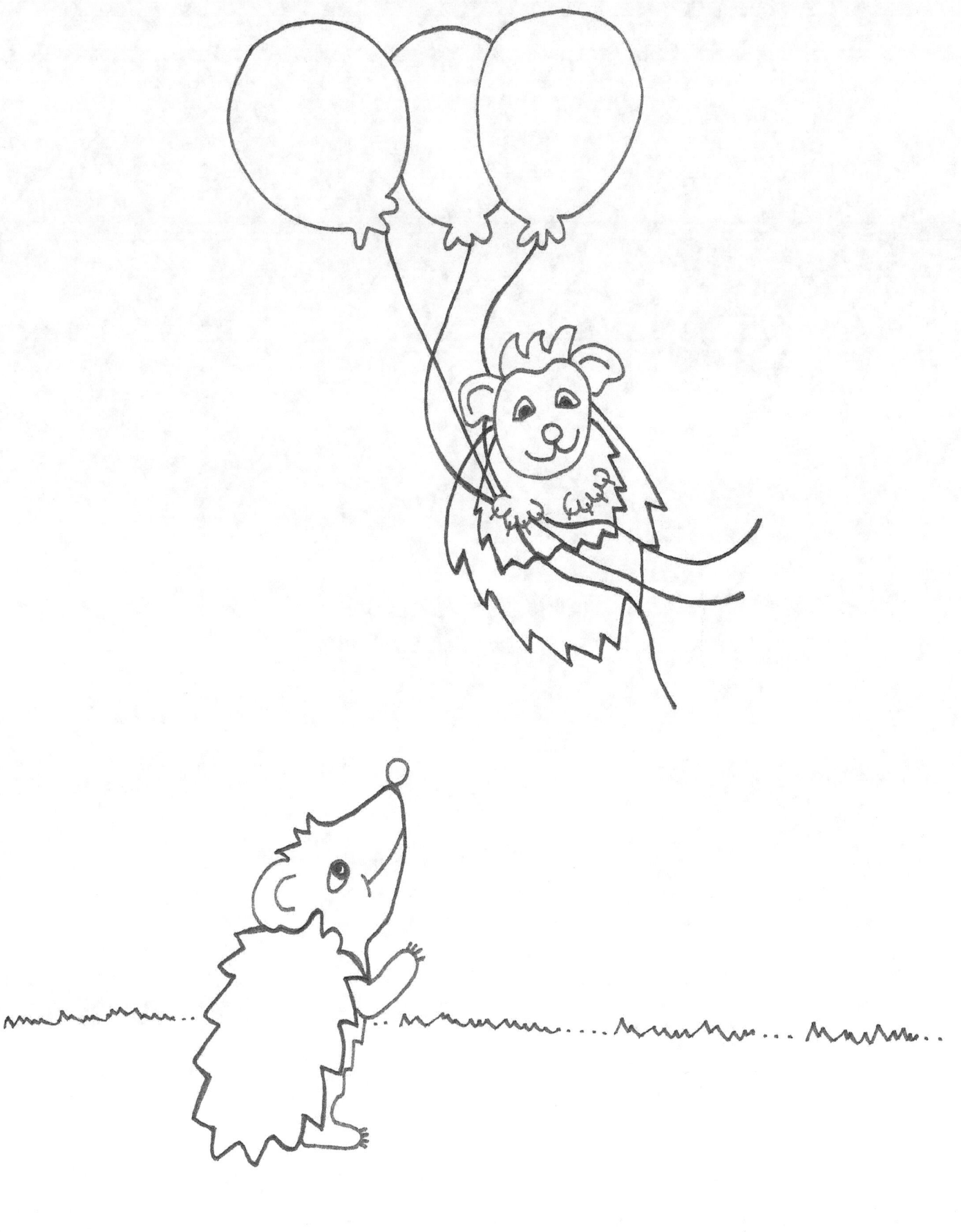

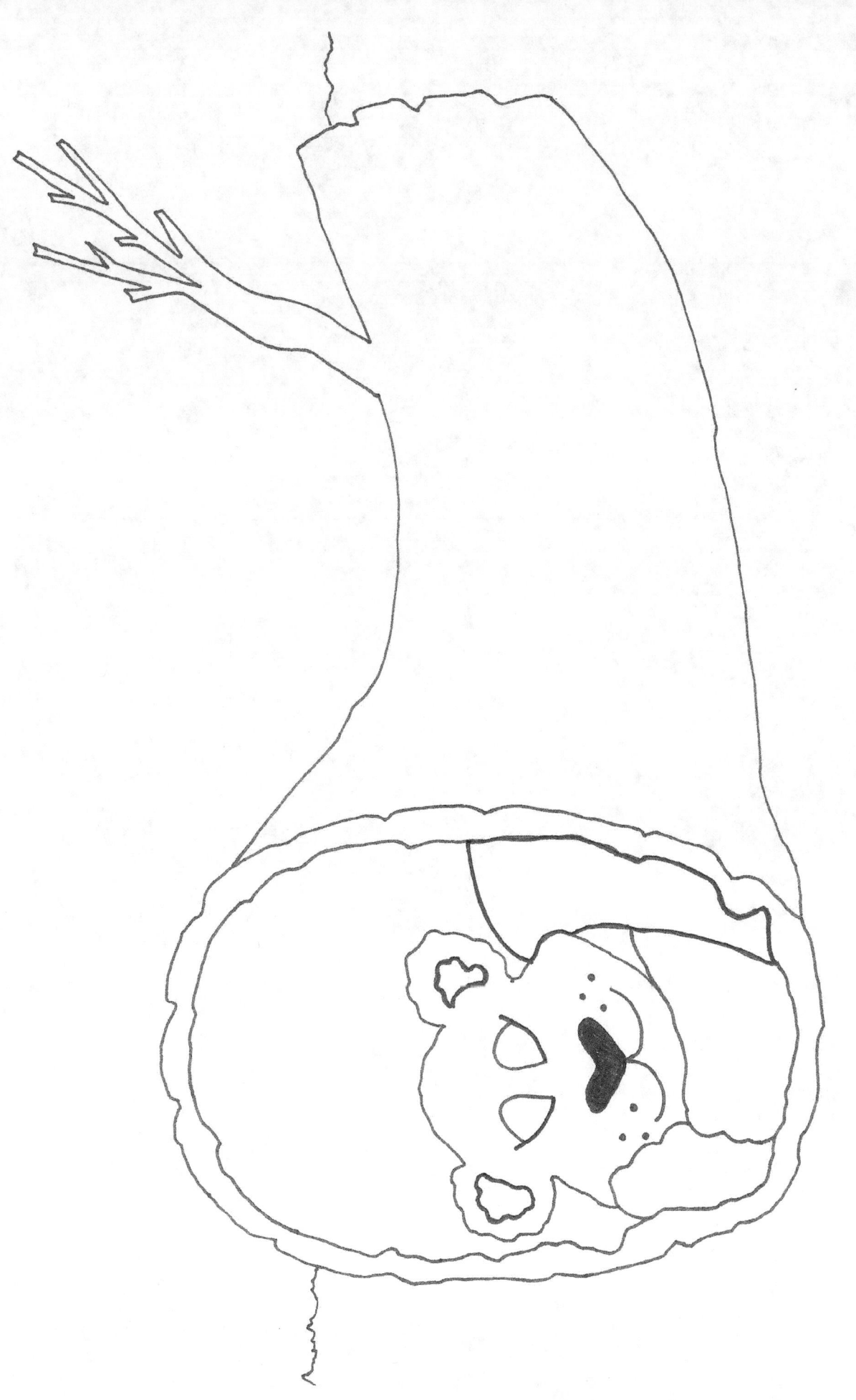

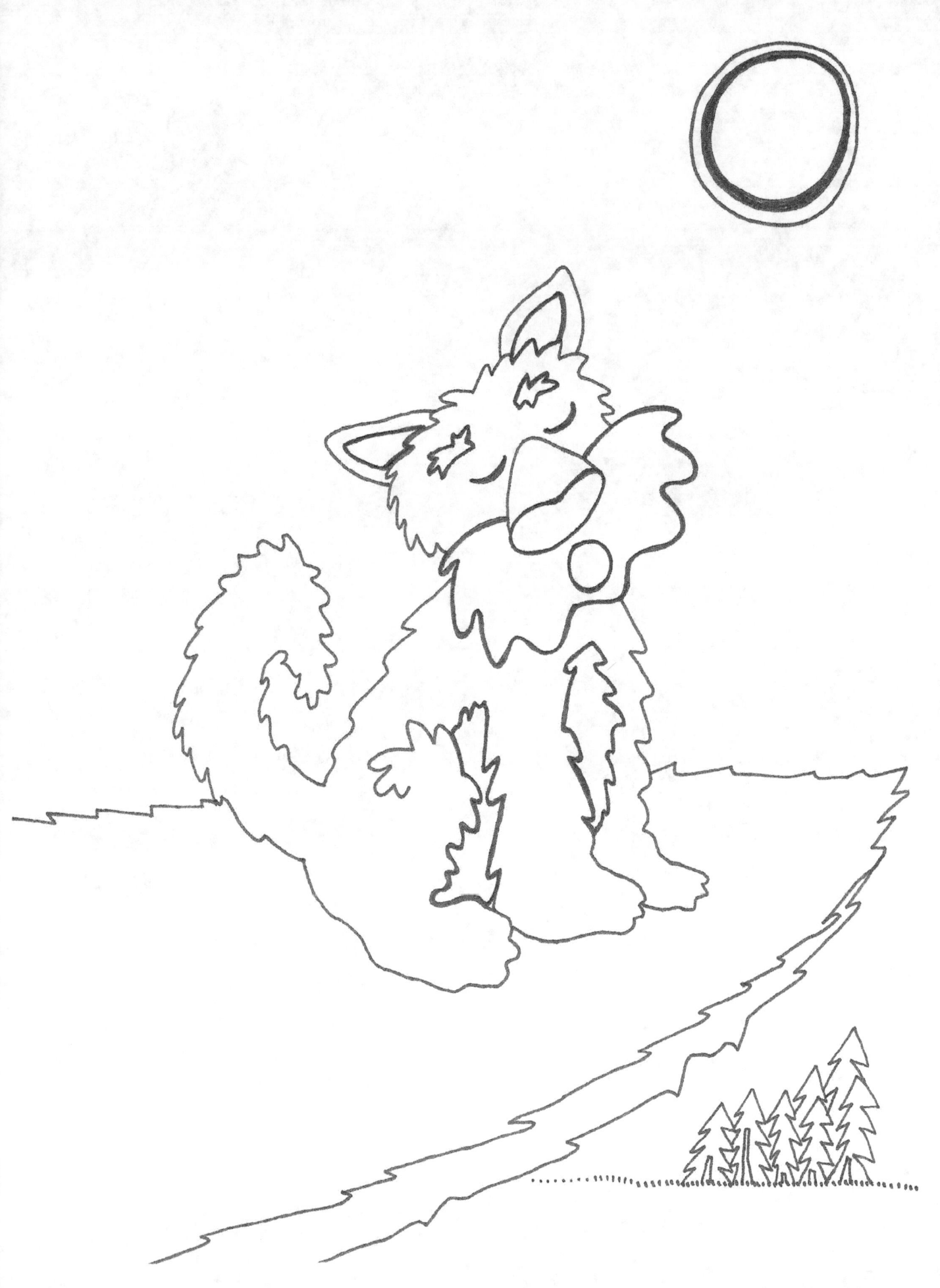

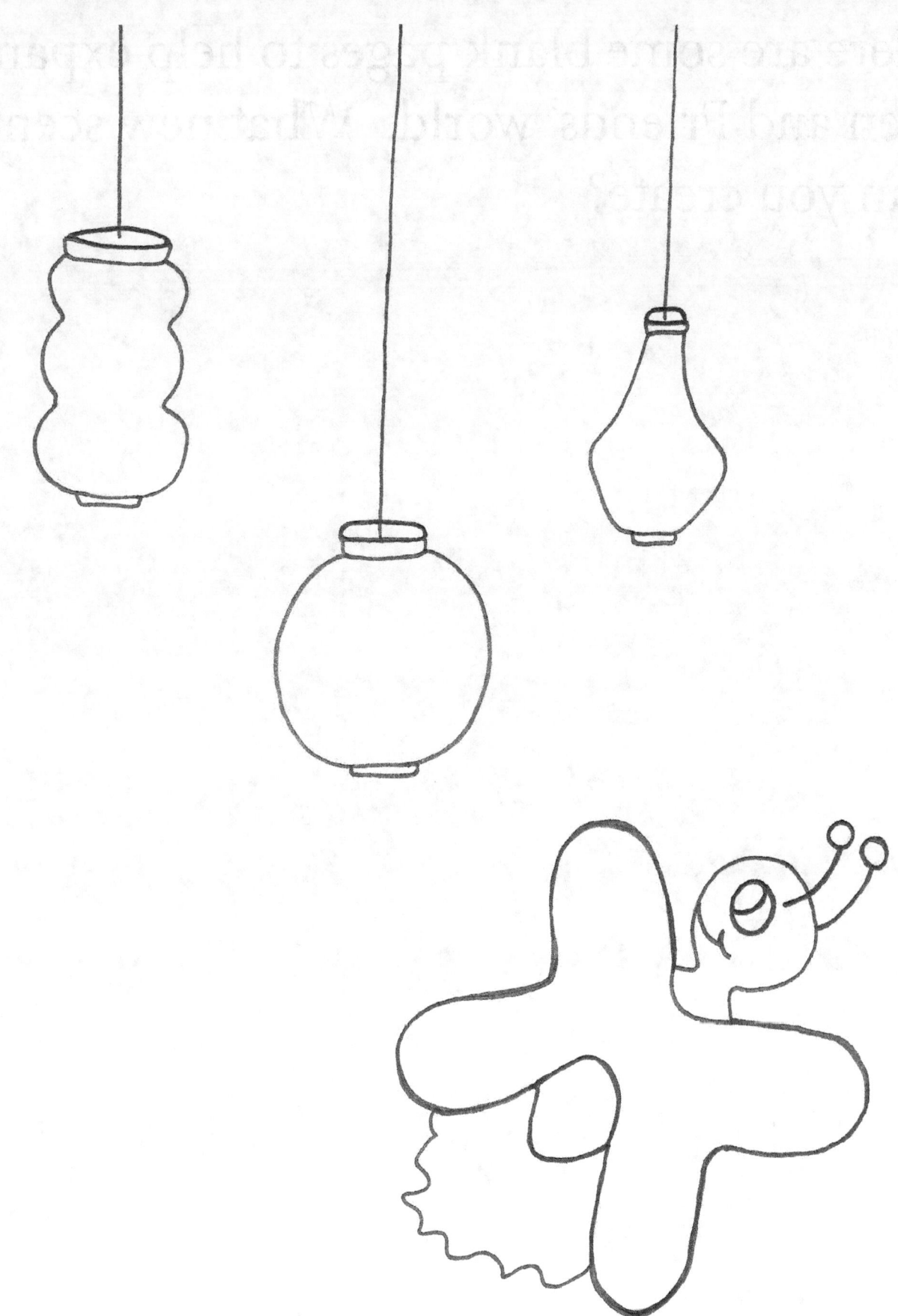

Here are some blank pages to help expand Zen and Friends' world. What new scenes can you create?

www.ingramcontent.com/pod-product-compliance
Lightning Source LLC
Chambersburg PA
CBHW080832170526
45158CB00009B/2552